CATHOLIC BUT NOT ROMAN, ORTHODOX BUT NOT EASTERN

[Document subtitle]

By

R. Joseph Owles

R. Joseph Owles

CATHOLIC BUT NOT ROMAN, ORTHODOX BUT
NOT EASTERN

Copyright © 2013

TABLE OF CONTENTS

You can find out more about The Old Catholic Church and Father R. Joseph Owles online at the following links:

http://kogcc.net

https://www.facebook.com/RJOwles

https://twitter.com/rjosephowles

http://www.writerscafe.org/rjowles

Protect us, Lord, as we stay awake; watch over us as we sleep, that awake, we may keep watch with Christ, and asleep, rest in his peace.

~ From the Office of Night Prayer

To All Who Ask;
To All Who Seek;
To All Who Knock.

CATHOLIC BUT NOT ROMAN; ORTHODOX BUT NOT EASTERN

What if there were a valid Catholic Church that allowed priests to marry, where divorce was not treated like an unforgiveable sin, where birth control and contraception were regarded as a personal decision and a matter of individual conscience, where divorced and remarried individuals were still allowed access to the Sacraments, where *EVERY* baptized individual were welcomed to receive the Eucharist, where women were ordained as deacons, priests, and bishops, and where you were welcomed just as you are, regardless of who you are? What if this Catholic Church maintained valid Apostolic Succession, administers valid Sacraments, and is guided by Holy Tradition and Holy Scripture – a church that is not Protestant or a "break away" church, but is *ONE HUNDRED PERCENT CATHOLIC* in its tradition, practice, and theology? What if such a Catholic Church existed? Would you be interested? Would you like to know more about it?

Such a Catholic Church does indeed exist!

It is The Old Catholic Church.

I am <u>Father R. Joseph Owles</u>. I am an Old Catholic priest. Much of my ministry has been providing Christian ministry for those who may not have access to a pastor or church ministry – for those people who may have fallen through the cracks. It has been a personal chaplaincy that seeks out and cares for those who have no particular church affiliation or church home. They may be Catholics who have been denied the Sacraments of the Church because of some situation such as divorce. They may be non-Christians who are looking for pastoral care, or traditional services such as weddings, funerals, and baptism.

My own personal ministry provides traditional, pastoral services to those in need, regardless of affiliation (or lack thereof) regardless of economic condition; regardless of circumstance. I often joke that I am like The A-Team – if you need pastoral care, pastoral services, someone to officiate a wedding, someone to administer the Sacraments, someone to officiate a funeral, someone to pray with you and for you, someone to hear your confession, or any other need, want, or desire that only ordained clergy can provide; and you can find me, then you can call me for ministry.

People who find me online, who meet me, who see me in action, or who attend weddings or funerals where I have officiated, often have questions. The common questions are "What is the Old Catholic Church?" and "How are you different from the Roman Catholic Church?" and "Why have I never heard of this church before?"

The purpose of this book is to serve as a brief introduction to The Old Catholic Church. Think of it as the "Frequently Asked Questions" section of ministry. It is an attempt to answer the common questions that I am routinely asked. This book is **_NOT_** written as an official statement or resource of any Old Catholic Church communion or jurisdiction. I am **_NOT_** the spokesperson for The Old Catholic Church. I am simply an Old Catholic priest answering questions and explaining **_MY UNDERSTANDING_** of what the Old Catholic Church is and the tradition from which it comes and on which it relies. Nevertheless, all the information presented in this book, unless otherwise noted, is the essence of the Old Catholic Tradition – a tradition that is remarkably orthodox and Catholic, yet, diverse and modern.

This book is intended to present the basics of The Old Catholic Church. In the following pages I will explain my understanding of what the Old Catholic Church is, where it comes from, what it believes, and how to learn more about it. You, the reader, will learn in modest detail that:

- The Old Catholic Church is not a product of the Reformation.

- The Old Catholic Church is not bound to the Bishop of Rome (although, we do respect the Bishop of Rome since he is a bishop and an heir to Apostolic authority).

- The Old Catholic Church is not monolithic in polity or structure; it is not centered in any one city or country.

- The Old Catholic Church defines Catholic Doctrine as those teachings passed down from generation to generation through Holy Scripture, Holy Tradition, and as defined in the Ecumenical Councils of the *WHOLE* (Catholic) Church.

- The Old Catholic Church maintains valid Apostolic Succession, valid Sacraments, and teaches Catholic beliefs.

- The Old Catholic Church is ecumenical – The Old Catholic Church works and plays well with other traditions and faiths.

You will learn that when it comes to *essential* Catholic teachings, The Old Catholic Church demonstrates unity. When it comes *to non-essential* Catholic teachings, The Old Catholic Church demonstrates liberty. In all our beliefs, The Old Catholic Church demonstrates charity. You will learn that it is a faith with a lot of freedom, while being traditionally Catholic – a faith that is summed up by many as:

A. All persons who have received a Trinitarian baptism are by virtue of that baptism Christians and Disciples of Christ.

B. All persons who have received a Trinitarian baptism and adhere to the ancient Catholic faith as expressed by the Nicene Creed are Catholics.

C. All persons who adhere to the full Catholic faith as received by the Church until the Schism of A.D. 1054 are Old Catholics, in the fullness of the Catholic faith.

D. All Christians holding the fullness of the Catholic and Apostolic faith, regardless of their church affiliation, are regarded as being in communion with us, and may be received in fellowship and admitted to the sacraments, and receive pastoral care.

Of course, this is a guide and not a rule. I use it to express our openness to Christians from other traditions. The short hand of this is: "If you show up, you are welcome! If you are baptized, you are welcome to come forward to take the Eucharist, regardless of your tradition." And I'm not standing up front during worship checking baptismal certificates.

If, when you finish this book, you find that you are interested in The Old Catholic Church and wish to learn more, then you will find a listing of Old Catholic Churches around the world. You will also find links to find me online if you are so moved to learn more about me as well as The Old Catholic Tradition.

May God Bless You in All That You Do

The Very Reverend R. Joseph Owles

WHAT DOES "CATHOLIC" MEAN?

Every week, in churches all over the world, Christians confess belief in "the catholic church." Some Christians do so by reciting the Apostles' Creed which confesses belief in "the holy catholic church," and others use the Nicene Creed which uses the phrase "one, holy, catholic, and apostolic church." Therefore, for the majority of the world's Christians, faith in a "catholic" church is a central part of their beliefs.

But what does the term "catholic" church mean? This surprisingly simple question has a surprisingly complicated answer. The fact is that there is a difference in how the word "catholic" is applied and what it means. There is certainly a difference between how the term is used today by most Christians and how it was used when it was first coined in the early second century. The simple truth for most Christians is that the "catholic Church" they confess each week probably does not mean what they think it means.

Protestant Christians understand that the word "catholic" simply means "universal." When they confess faith in the catholic church, they are confessing that there is one Church in many forms and expressions, and that they are a part of that one church. This understanding is a fairly recent development in the use of the word. For much of Protestantism, there was an understanding in which each Protestant tradition taught that it was the only valid Church. Toward the end of the twentieth century, Protestantism shifted from this historical exclusive use of the word "catholic" (as in "We are the true Church, and other expressions of Christianity are false") to a more inclusive use (as in "We are part of the universal church along with other expressions of Christianity.")

Roman Catholics use the word "catholic" as designating those churches that are fully united with the Bishop of Rome. When they confess faith in the catholic church, it is an explicit faith in "The Catholic Church," meaning "The Roman Catholic Church." The Catholic Church, then, is an organizational structure, as well as dogma and practices that flow from that structure. The CEO of this structure is the Bishop of Rome (commonly referred to as "The Pope"), who is also the ruler of a nation called The Vatican. Roman Catholics have been so successful in redefining the term that for the most part, at least in Western Christianity, the term "Catholic" has become synonymous with "Roman Catholic."

What Protestants and Roman Catholics have in common is that structure appears to be the essence of what they both mean when they use the word "catholic." Roman Catholics are more explicit about this in that the very definition of who is catholic and who is not is essentially identical with who is a member of a church united with the Bishop of Rome and who is not. Yet, the very idea of the "universal" church that Protestants confess is also implicitly structural. There is an entity called "The Church" and Protestant churches claim to be a part of that universal entity. Therefore, in Western Christianity, for the most part, The Church is an institution, a structure, an organization, that is either defined from the top down (Pope to pew) or the bottom up (congregation of believers).

The word "catholic," however, initially did not refer to structure, or polity, or organization, but to faith. It was neither a structure flowing from the Pope, nor was it a congregation of believers, but it was a community of faith. It is the faith that is catholic, not the structure. The structure, or institution, or polity, is catholic because it shares in, and is founded on, the catholic faith.

The word "catholic" is a compound word constructed from two Greek words: *kata* (according to) and *holos* (whole). Catholic means "according to the whole," and the catholic Church means "according to the whole Church." The "universal" quality of the word "catholic" is not a universal Church, but a universal faith which identifies the Church. The Church exemplifies the catholic faith — the faith that is everywhere in the whole Church. The phrase first arose as a response to heresy.

One of the first heresies to develop (alluded to in the Epistles of John) was the idea that Jesus Christ was not truly a human being, but merely appeared to be human. This idea became known as Docetism (from the Greek *dokein* "to appear"). In this view, Jesus was, in reality, a spiritual being who took human appearance, but who was in no way authentically or biologically human. Some extreme forms of this teaching asserted that Jesus' feet did not even touch the ground, but that he floated above the earth as he walked. The conclusion of this teaching meant that the spiritual being in human disguise known as Jesus could not experience pain because pain is physical, and since Jesus was purely spiritual, he free from the incumbrances of the physical world. Therefore, there can be no crucifixion, or Passion, or even birth for that matter. The concept of the catholic Church became a useful tool to combat such heresies. The practical application was simple: "You say that Jesus was a spiritual being who was not human, but the Church everywhere else says Jesus was born of a woman, suffered under Pontius Pilate, was crucified, died, and was buried." "According to your church, you say that Jesus was not a physical being, but according to the whole Church, Jesus was so physical that he was born, experienced pain, and died."[1]

---

[1] One can see how the Nicene Creed and the Apostles Creed developed to confront heresies such as Docetism and Gnosticism. Justo L. Gonzalez in *The Story of Christianity, Vol. 1* asserts that the Church's response to the heresies that developed in the second century was the development of three things: catholic, creed, and apostolic succession.

So the term "catholic" is not simply "universal," but it is a particular kind of universal. It is not the universal church, but the universal faith of the Church. The definition of "catholic," then, as stated by St. Vincent of Lerins (in 434), is "that faith which has been believed everywhere, always, by all." St. Vincent of Lerins goes on to say: "We shall follow universality if we confess that one faith to be true, which the whole Church throughout the world confesses."

Therefore, when Christians confess faith in the catholic church, they may be contradicting what the phrase "catholic Church" means. Faith in a structure united with the Bishop of Rome may not be in keeping with what the Church has always taught in all places. Faith in a universal church that is made up of a collection of very different churches that believe different things may not be in keeping with what the Church has always taught in all places. The matter becomes even more complicated when contemporary churches and traditions revise historical doctrines and teachings to match contemporary understandings. It only exacerbates the situation when a church or tradition asserts that it is *THE* True Church or *THE* Catholic Church to the exclusion of others.

So how do we know what the Catholic faith is that was always taught and believed in all places? Many Christians suggest that the catholic faith is the faith expressed by the Church through Holy Scripture, Apostolic Tradition, the teachings of the Church Fathers, and the rulings of Ecumenical Councils of the whole Church (which occurred before the schism in 1054).

The holy catholic Church is not a structure or any particular denomination or jurisdiction. It is a Community of Faith – or perhaps more correctly, it is a faith around which a community gathers. It is not a gathering of people who identify as Christian or a particular kind of Christian. It is not a gathering of those who share a specific type of structure or polity. It is not a congregation of those who are believers. It is a community that gathers around the faith taught in the Bible, explained through the Apostles, bishops, and teachers of the early Church, and which has been clarified by the seven gatherings of the whole Church which met before Eastern and Western Christianity split (and excommunicated each other) in 1054.

WHAT DOES "CHURCH" MEAN?

The English word "church" is derived from the Greek compound word *kyriakon* which never appears in the Bible. It is made from *kyrios* (Lord) and *oikos* (house). The meaning of *kyriakon* is "the Lord's house" – a term that is still in use by many Christians who refer to a church building as "the Lord's house" or "God's house." As mentioned, this word is never used anywhere in the Bible and when early-Christians spoke of "the church," they were never referring to a building or a house belonging to God, the Lord, or anyone else.

The word that is translated as "church" in the New Testament is *ekklesia*. The word means "those who are called out"; "chosen people"; "the elect." It is the word that appears in the Septuagint (the Greek translation of the Hebrew Scriptures) for the gathered people of Israel.

The point is simple: *kyriakon* is a building; *ekklesia* is people. The idea of the Church being a structure or a building is not the New Testament understanding of the word church. Unfortunately, this idea has replaced the biblical meaning of church found in the New Testament. The Church is not the Lord's house, but it is the Lord's people.

The New Testament never uses the adjectives "catholic" or "universal" when referring to the church.

Nevertheless, authors such as Paul indicate that local communities are all united even though they are different and dispersed. The people in these churches are to live in harmony with each other and we members of other church communities. Division is to be avoided, and those who cause division must be corrected or shunned until they change. The New Testament expresses the idea that each of these individual congregations is working together to spread the Gospel to all nations throughout the whole earth. The New Testament also makes it clear that these communities are to be open to all people. Therefore, even if the word "catholic" does not appear in the Bible, the concept of "catholic" is expressed in the New Testament (at least in kit form with some assembly required).

Keeping in mind of what has already been said about the meanings of the words "disciple" and "catholic," a definition of "the Church" may be offered. The Church is "the collection of people chosen by God to be disciples, to adhere to the catholic[2] faith expressed in the Gospel (good news) of Jesus Christ, and to communicate that Gospel through words and deeds to the ends of the earth."

When we remember that the best understanding of the word "disciple" is that of "apprentice," then we must conclude that those who are chosen by God to be disciples are not necessarily chosen to be winners of some divine lottery or to receive some unique essence or quality that

---

[2] Refer to section: "What Does 'Catholic' Mean?"

sets them above others. They are chosen to be apprentices of Jesus Christ. They are chosen by God to learn from Jesus how to be like Jesus. This learning to be like Jesus is not to serve themselves, but it is so they can present Jesus to others, some of whom will become fellow-apprentices. Just as the Son of Man did not come to be served, but to serve, and to give his life as a ransom to many, so to those who are chosen to be disciples will also give their lives to the service of others.

The meaning of all this is that we do not GO TO church, but we *ARE* the Church. The consequence of that may be that the people who *ARE* the Church may meet together in the building that is *A* church. But the people meeting together in that building may not all be *THE* Church.

WHAT IS THE OLD CATHOLIC CHURCH?

The Old Catholic Church is neither Protestant, nor is it the product of the Reformation. It is not a group of Catholics who broke away from the Roman Catholic Church to start its own church. If anything, the Old Catholic Church regards the Roman Catholic Church as the church that broke away—hence the name "Old" Catholic. Conversely, the Roman Catholic Church considers the Old Catholic Churches to be in "schism."[3]

The original geographic center for the Church was Jerusalem. The Bible makes that much clear. Yet, other religious centers soon emerged in Antioch, Alexandria, and elsewhere including Rome. When Constantine made Christianity a legal religion in the Roman Empire, and then later favored it, Constantinople became the Christian geographical center. The Councils confirmed Constantinople and Jerusalem as the primary centers of Christianity, and listed Antioch, Alexandria, and Rome as secondary in importance.

Nevertheless, even though the Christian Church was centered in Constantinople, the Roman bishop began asserting that he was the head of the church. This, of course, was annoying to the head of the church in

---

[3] The issue that caused the schism in the church was that of Papal Infallibility, which was also linked to the Doctrine of the Immaculate Conception. (More about that later).

Constantinople. The claim of the Roman bishop was largely ignored. This remained the case until the fall of the Western Empire in 476. The Empire continued in the East, and since Rome was no longer the capital (it had not been since Diocletian moved the Capital to Nikomedia in Asia Minor in the 280s), the loss of the Western Empire was viewed to be important only in terms of lost territory. Roman civilization had moved to the East and was firmly centered in, Constantinople. This included the church as well.

The church based in Rome began to grow in influence in Europe when the Franks began to conquer the surrounding Germanic peoples. This happened for two reasons. The first was that the Roman church expanded to fill the vacuum left by the decline and absence of Roman administration. The second was that the Frankish King wanted to be called Emperor, but there was no longer an emperor in the West. Before the fall of the Western Empire, an emperor was set up in Rome to help manage the empire. The Roman emperor was not an equal to the Emperor in Constantinople. To the contrary, the Roman emperor was his subordinate. The importance of this, however, is that a tradition of *TWO* emperors had been established. Since there was no longer an emperor in Rome, there was a vacancy for the position for a Western emperor. The Frankish king was eager to fill that vacancy.

The Roman bishop worked out a deal with the Frankish king–if the king of the Franks would recognize the Bishop of Rome as the head of the church in his Frankish "Empire," then the Bishop of Rome would crown him as Emperor. This agreement caused additional friction between the Western and Eastern versions of the then one church centered in Constantinople. This and other sources of friction would eventually lead to a split of the one church into two churches–the Eastern Orthodox Churches in the East, and the Roman Catholic Church in the West.

By now you are wondering what any of this has to do with the development of the Old Catholic Church. To that I can only counsel: "Patience, Grasshopper. I am getting to it." The Old Catholic Church is a product of the Roman Catholic Church in the Netherlands. The Netherlands were viewed as out in the wilderness of Europe, especially from the point of view of Rome. The result was that the church in the Netherlands was used to being on its own and taking care of itself. The Dutch church was viewed by the church based in Rome as independent, and publicly and officially said so in 1125 when the Bishop of Rome decreed it independent and granted it the right to name and ordain its own bishops, making the Bishop of Utrecht the head of the Dutch Catholic Church and empowering him to handle the affairs of the Dutch church. This was confirmed by the Fourth Lateran Council which met in 1215.

CATHOLIC BUT NOT ROMAN, ORTHODOX BUT NOT EASTERN

The Old Catholic Church arose from that Independent Catholic Church in The Netherlands. So, once more, it is not a break-away church or a Reformation church, but it was born in the church that was granted authority to be independent by the Roman Pontiff himself. The Dutch Catholic Church was a legitimate expression of Catholicism in the West according to the Roman Catholic Church; therefore, the Old Catholic Church which stems from the church in the Netherlands is also a legitimate expression of Catholicism.[4]

---

[4] It is true that some Roman Catholics walked out of the First Vatican Council and asked to join the Dutch Catholic Church, but the church itself that they joined had existed since Christianity had arrived in that region, and the church they joined was always independent, having that independence unequivocally declared by the Roman Pontiff himself as early as 1125.

WHY ISN'T THE "OLD" CATHOLIC CHURCH THE "ROMAN" CATHOLIC CHURCH?

If the Old Catholic Church is not some break-away group or Protestant church, why isn't it "Roman" Catholic? The Roman Catholic Church has a history of "breaking away." First, it broke away from the church that was centered in Constantinople, then, and as far as Old Catholics are concerned, it broke away from itself.

Remember, the Roman Catholic Church considers the Old Catholic Churches to be in schism. They also consider the Eastern Orthodox Churches to be in schism as well. Schism means that Old Catholics are not "heretics" (as Protestants technically are according to the Roman Catholic Church), but the Old Catholic Churches are not in communion, or full communion with Rome, and as a result, cannot be "Catholic."

The Roman Catholic Church has essentially rebranded the meaning of the word "Catholic" so that it no longer holds to its original meaning of "what was taught by the Church in all times and places." The Roman Catholic understanding of the word "Catholic" now simply means: "being in union with the Bishop of Rome." Therefore, to be "Catholic" in the Roman Catholic Church's use of the world is to be under the authority of the Bishop of Rome, which in itself is a violation of the original meaning of the word

"Catholic" since the universal authority of the Bishop of Rome was not taught in all times and in all places, but it is a new idea that is unique to the Roman Catholic.[5]

Nevertheless, the issue that generated the "schism" between the Roman Catholic Church and the Old Catholic Church was not simply the differing and irreconcilable understandings of the world "Catholic." A conflict over doctrine let to the split. The doctrinal issue that fostered the schism was that of Papal Infallibility, which was in itself the result of the Doctrine of the Immaculate Conception.

The Doctrine of the Immaculate Conception is the teaching that the Blessed Virgin Mary was born without Original Sin so that she could become the Mother of our Lord Jesus Christ. Original Sin is the sinful nature passed down to all humanity from Adam and Eve. It is the product of The Fall. The sin of the first parents was passed down to all their children, and their children's children, and so on, down to the present generation of human beings.

The Doctrine of Original Sin states that we are stained by the sin of our first parents even before we ourselves commit any sin of thought, word, or deed. The Immaculate Conception was presented as a logical line of reasoning to explain how Jesus could be free from sin, yet born of a

---

[5] Therefore, the "Old" in the Old Catholic Church is linked to the idea that we hold to the Old (as in original) understanding of what the word "Catholic" means.

woman who would have been stained by Original Sin. Either Original Sin is passed down through the male, or Mary must have somehow been free of that sin in order to give birth to Jesus, who was free from all sin – original and otherwise.

In the year 1476, Pope Sixtus IV established a feast day for the Immaculate Conception. This was his right to do. Members of the Roman Catholic Church were left to themselves to decide if this was something they wanted to accept. The doctrine was not forced on anyone, and that is how it remained for nearly four hundred years.

This changed in 1854, when Pope Pius IX declared that the Immaculate Conception was a dogma of the church. The pope ordered Catholics to accept the Immaculate Conception as a central doctrine of the church. He decided that the doctrine was infallible; therefore, all Catholics must accept it. When asked why he considered the doctrine infallible, he answered that it was infallible because he could speak without error on such matters of church doctrine. This was new. No pope, nor anyone else had claimed the ability to issue infallible doctrine.

The logic of the pope was simply I can assert that the Doctrine of the Immaculate Conception is a central and infallible teaching of the church because I am infallible when speaking on doctrinal matters. In essence, the pope simply stated: "The doctrine is infallible because I say so, and because I say so, it is infallible." So, what had begun as a debate about whether one was required to accept and acknowledge the Feast of the Immaculate Conception, morphed into a debate on whether the pope is infallible on matters of doctrine.

The schism between Old Catholics and Roman Catholics occurred because a pope wanted to force all Catholics to accept the Doctrine of the Immaculate Conception, which was not an ancient doctrine taught by the Church in all places but was a purely Western idea that was only about four hundred years old at the time. When challenged about doing that, he countered by declaring himself infallible on matters of doctrine. It was a circular logic: since the pope was infallible on matters of doctrine, the pope could infallibly declare himself to be infallible; and after declaring himself infallible, he could then declare that the optional Feast of the Immaculate Conception be required by all Catholics as a core component to Christian faith.

This did not happen without a fight. A group of bishops met together at the First Vatican Council to discuss this and other matters. It soon became apparent that the council was stacked with Italian bishops who supported the decree of the Italian pope. When it became evident that Papal Infallibility was going to pass regardless of debate and dissent, a group of bishops walked out. That is why the issue passed by nearly unanimous consent – all the bishops who opposed it walked out before the vote.

Many of the bishops who walked out of the First Vatican Council went to the Catholic Church in the Netherlands, which was officially independent even though it was Catholic, and asked to join their communion. Thus, the Old Catholic Church was born, and it is also why they call themselves "Old" Catholics, as opposed to those "New" Catholics who accept new doctrines and dogmas like the Immaculate Conception and Papal Infallibility.

So again, the Old Catholic Church never broke away from anyone. If anyone broke away, Old Catholics feel it is the Roman Catholic Church – it broke away from its own history and tradition to grant infallible power to the Bishop of Rome and remove it from Ecumenical Councils, which the Catholic Church – the whole Catholic Church, not just the Roman version of it – has always affirmed.

IF THE POPE ISN'T "INFALLIBLE," WHAT IS?

Perhaps it may be silly to even utter a word like "infallibility" in a time when we have access to more information than any other period of history—and that increased information seems to produce and debunk and reproduce new ideas and "facts" every day (or even many times a day). Maybe the word we are searching for, or would be more comfortable with, is *"RELIABLE"* rather than *"INFALLIBLE"* Nevertheless, infallible is the word that was used, and it is a word still in use by Protestants as well as Roman Catholics.

Some Protestants use the word "infallible" when talking about the Bible. The information in the Bible is inerrant. By this they mean that the Bible is completely factually and historically accurate. They are not simply saying that the Bible is true in that the ideas that it expresses are true. They are saying that it is factual in that it is objectively certain and contains no errors. Even after thousands of years of copying by hand the books of the Bible (often by hearing it read, and writing what was heard), it contains no errors.

If anyone wants to accept the idea that the Bible is inerrant, then that is fine. Everyone has the right to assert and believe whatever makes them happy. But when Protestants offer this idea to Catholics who have some knowledge of history and tradition, it usually raises a question: If the Bible really is infallible, why then did Protestants start stripping away books from the Bible when those books presented doctrines that the Reformers did not like? When and how did those books of the Bible become fallible? Martin Luther did not like the Book of Esther and especially hated the Epistle of James. He wanted them taken out of the Bible. He failed in his attempt, so they remained "infallible"; but would they have suddenly been "fallible" if he succeeded?

Luther and other Reformers did have a logical and historical way of dealing with most of the books they did not like. Esther and James aside, most of the books were those that are commonly termed deuterocanonical by Catholics and called apocryphal by Protestants. These are books that were part of the Septuagint (the Greek translation of the Old Testament) but which had fallen away from the Hebrew translations of the Old Testament. The Greek Old Testament was the version used by most of the Church, so these extra books were part of the Christian tradition. When Jerome was translating the Bible into Latin, he questioned the validity of some of these books, but he did not feel as if he alone had the authority to dismiss them. So he decided to group these books together and place them in a section between the Old and New Testaments – a practice often followed to this day. Luther and other Reformers revived the practice of placing these books as a separate grouping and denied they had any doctrinal authority. They eventually fell away from most Protestant Bibles.

Digression aside, the point is that the idea of the Bible being infallible is a relatively new idea in the life of the Church and is largely a Protestant idea and the Product of the Reformation. The Reformers needed a logical means of justifying their views since they sought to undermine the teaching authority of the church. The authority they arrived at was *Sola Scriptura*, "Scripture alone." This meant that the Scripture had to become inerrant so that they could then use it as the basis of their Scripture alone doctrine.[6]

Protestants came up with the idea of "infallible" before the Roman Pontiff did. The Reformers who broke away from the Catholic Church used the idea of biblical infallibility to justify their rejection of Catholicism. So, it should not have been surprising when a couple of centuries later, a pope decided to make himself infallible. If a Reformer rejecting Catholicism and creating a new church could declare the Bible infallible (even though no one had done that before), why not a pope, who is the head administrator and arbiter of the church, not declare himself infallible (even though no one had done that before)?

---

[6] The doctrine of *Sola Scriptura* is nowhere found in Scripture; therefore, the doctrine of *Sola Scriptura* violates the principle of *Sola Scriptura*.

The Old Catholic response to both is the same: If anything is infallible, it is the series of decisions laid down by the Ecumenical Councils of the Church. This is a fancy way of saying Old Catholics assert that the authority for reliable doctrine and dogma is church councils, but not just any church councils, but only those councils made up of the whole (or catholic) church. This means that Old Catholics subscribe to the idea that was taken for granted until the Reformers started declaring that the Bible is infallible, and the pope started declaring that he was infallible, that infallibility lies in the entire church meeting together in a church-wide (or ecumenical) council to debate and decide the issue under the guidance of the Holy Spirit.

This is not a radical idea! This is what the church said and agreed to until the 1500s when Reformers decided for themselves what was doctrine, and then in the 1800s when the pope decided that he was infallible and able to issue doctrine. But for 1500 years, the church settled matters of doctrine and dogma by meeting together in councils, and whatever the council decided settled the issue. This is what Old Catholics still believe in—ecumenical councils to establish church doctrine and dogma.

There is, however, a wrinkle to this belief: no ecumenical council has been possible since 1054. That is the year that the Eastern and Western Churches split, dividing the One Church into two churches—the Eastern

Orthodox Churches and the Roman Catholic Church. These two churches then began to disintegrate into hundreds or thousands of churches beginning in 1517 when Martin Luther unwittingly kicked off the Reformation. Therefore, true ecumenical councils are extremely difficult to initiate and unlikely to occur.

By now, someone may be asking: "If Old Catholics believe in doctrine that is derived by ecumenical councils, then why did they not accept the decisions of the First Vatican Council? The answer is that The First Vatican Council was not an ecumenical council of the whole church but was in fact a synod of the Roman Catholic Church. It did not include bishops and priests from Eastern Orthodox Churches, or from Protestant Churches, or any other part of the Church. It was purely Roman Catholics mainly from Europe. So, it was *NOT* an ecumenical council. At best ot was a synod of part of the Church—the Roman Catholic Part.

An Old Catholic would most likely assert that the Roman Catholic Church has the authority in that or any other synod to declare that for Roman Catholics, the Doctrines of the Immaculate Conception, and the Infallibility of the Pope, and whatever other doctrine it wants to assert, must be accepted, but that does not make those doctrines infallible truths for the whole church, or *THE* Catholic Church. Only those teachings decided upon by the whole Church established before the split in 1054 can be understood as core doctrines for the *WHOLE* Church.

So Old Catholics accept the Roman Catholic Church's right to create new-fangled, fancy doctrines for itself, but it does not have the right to assert that others outside the Roman Catholic Church accept those newly created doctrines unless those doctrines pass the test of being accepted by an ecumenical council, not a Roman Catholic Synod like the First Vatican Council.

Old Catholics say (as the church has always said) that there have been seven Ecumenical Councils of the Church. This means that since the word "catholic" means "the Church everywhere" and that "ecumenical" means the "whole" church, then these seven ecumenical councils of the whole church declared the teaching of the church for Christians everywhere and thus define true universal (Catholic) Christianity.

The Seven Ecumenical Councils of the Early Church:

Council of Nicaea, 325

The first council of Nicaea rejected the heresy of Arianism, which held that Christ is a creature less than God the Father. The council declared that Christ is *"of the same substance with the Father"* and *"God from God."* The Son is co-eternal with the Father. It also adopted the Nicene Creed (though not the complete version of the Nicene Creed used today), established the date for celebrating Easter, recognized Rome, Alexandria, and Antioch as important jurisdictions, granted the See of Jerusalem a place of special honor.

Council of Constantinople, 381

This council declared that Christ is fully human with a human soul. The council also stated that the Holy Spirit is worshiped and glorified with the Father and the Son. The Father is the source, the Son is begotten, and the Holy Spirit proceeds from the Father. Made changes to the Nicene Creed in regards to the Holy Spirit, which became the Nicene Creed that is used in churches during worship and accepted by most Christian traditions and denominations as an authoritative statement of the Christian faith. The council also condemned Apollinarism which taught that Christ has no human mind or soul in Christ but that he was completely a divine Spirit in a human body.

Council of Ephesus, 431

The Council of Ephesus condemned the teachings of Nestorius who taught that Christ did not only possess two natures but was, in fact, two persons – one human, and one divine. It also condemned Pelagianism, a teaching that states that there is no Original Sin and we can achieve salvation on our own good acts and works. It proclaimed the Virgin Mary as *Theotokos* ("God-Bearer," or "Mother of God"). It also reaffirmed the Nicene Creed.

Council of Chalcedon, 451

The council rejected Monophysitism, which taught that Christ only had one nature and that Christ's human nature was absorbed by the divine nature. It declared that the divine and human natures of Christ are permanently united, but without being mixed or confused or changed into some third entity. The council concluded that Jesus Christ is truly God and truly human and stated this in the Chalcedonian Creed. It established the Sees of Constantinople and Jerusalem as patriarchates, making them the primary jurisdictions of Christianity.

Second Council of Constantinople, 553

This council reaffirmed the church's teaching regarding the two natures of Christ and corrected certain misunderstandings of the teaching, such as Nestorianism that taught that Christ did not only possess two natures but was, in fact, two persons – one human and one divine. The Catholic Church taught and teaches that Christ has two natures but is one person. It condemned the teachings of Origen of Alexandria, and it decreed that only one person of the Trinity suffered in the flesh.

Third Council of Constantinople, 680-681

This council condemned Monothelitism which taught that although Christ had two natures (human and divine), he only had one divine will. The council asserted that the two natures of Christ carried out their own independent wills without conflict or confusion.

Council of Nicaea, 787

This council, which met in Nicaea, declared that images of Jesus Christ could be made and used in worship since Jesus Christ, in addition to being God is also human and human beings can be depicted in art. This ended the Iconoclast Controversy that taught that using images in worship was   wrong and destroyed religious art. Icons can be used and venerated according to the whole church.

The Creeds

The ecumenical councils presented and refined a creed known as the Nicene Creed which expresses the foundation upon which the doctrines and dogmas of the church are based. It is used to this day by Christians in worship. It states (my translation):

The Nicene Creed (381)

We believe in one God, the All-Governing Father, Creator of heaven and earth, and of everything that is visible and invisible.

And in one Lord, Jesus Christ, the uniquely-born Son of God, who was born of the Father before this age began, light from light, true God from true God, fathered, not made, of one substance with the Father; through him, all things were made. For us and for our salvation, he came down from heaven, became flesh by the Holy Spirit and the Virgin Mary, and became human. For our sake he was crucified under Pontius Pilate; he suffered death and was buried. On the third day, he rose again in accordance with the Scriptures; he ascended into heaven and is seated at the right hand of the Father. He will come again in glory to judge the living and the dead, and his kingdom will have no end.

And [we believe] in the Holy Spirit, the Lord, the giver of life, who proceeds from the Father [and the Son], who with the Father and the Son is worshiped and glorified, who has spoken through the prophets.

[We believe] in one, holy, catholic, and apostolic Church. We acknowledge one baptism for the forgiveness of sins. We look for the resurrection of the dead, and the life of the world to come. Amen.

CATHOLIC BUT NOT ROMAN, ORTHODOX BUT NOT EASTERN

The version of the Nicene Creed used in worship is one that was amended by later councils. The Creed produced by the First Council at Nicaea is as follows:

The Original Nicene Creed From The Council of Nicaea (325)

We believe in one God, the All-Governing Father, Creator of everything, visible and invisible.

We believe in one Lord Jesus Christ, the Son of God, born from the Father, [that is, uniquely-born from the substance of the Father, God from God], light from light, true God from true God, born, not made, of the same substance as the Father.

Through Him, all things were made [both in heaven and on earth].

The one who, for us humans, and for our salvation, came down and became flesh, and was made human.

He suffered, and was resurrected on the third day, and ascended into heaven. He is coming again to judge the living and the dead.

And in the Holy Spirit.

[But those who say: "There was a time when he was not," and "He was not before he was born," and "He was made out of nothing," or "He is of a different substance or essence," or who assert that the Son of God is "created," or "changeable," or "alterable," are condemned by the holy, catholic, and apostolic Church.]

The Council at Chalcedon also produced a creed or statement.

Chalcedonian Creed

In being of one accord with what the Holy Fathers taught, we teach people to confess the one and only Son, our Lord Jesus Christ, who is equally perfect in Godhead and also perfect in humanity. He is truly God and truly human, possessing a rational soul and body. He is of the same substance with the Father according to the Godhead, and of the same substance with us according to our humanness. He is like us in every way, but without sin. He was born of the Father before all ages according to the Godhead. In these latter days, for us and for our salvation, he was born of the Virgin Mary, the God-Bearer, according to our humanness.

He is the one and only Christ, Son, Lord, the uniquely-born, all of which are recognized in two natures, which are without confusion, without changing one into the other, without dividing them, and without separating them into different categories. The distinction of the two separate natures is in no way eliminated by the union, but rather, the properties of each nature is preserved, and coexist in one Person and one Subsistence. He is not parted or divided into two persons, but the one and only Son and the uniquely-born Word of God, the Lord Jesus Christ. It is exactly what we were taught about him from the beginning by the prophets, by what the Lord Jesus Christ himself has taught us, and by the Creed that the Holy Fathers has passed down to us.

In addition to the Nicene Creed which is used in worship by Christians to this day. The Catholic traditions of the Church also accepts the Apostles' Creed, also known as the Baptismal Creed because of its use during baptisms, and the Athanasian Creed which defines the doctrine of the Trinity.

The Apostles' Creed

I believe in God, the all-governing Father, who created heaven and earth.

And in Jesus Christ, his uniquely-born Son, our Lord. The one who was conceived by the Holy Spirit; who was born of Mary, the virgin; who suffered under Pontius Pilate; who was crucified, died and was buried; who descended the realm of the dead; who was resurrected from the dead on the third day; who ascended into heaven; who sits at the right hand of God, the All-Powerful Father; from there he is coming to judge the living and the dead.

I believe in the Holy Spirit, the holy catholic church, the fellowship of the holy ones, the forgiveness of sins, the resurrection of the flesh, and eternal life. Amen.

The Athanasian Creed

Whoever wants to be saved must, above all else, adhere to the catholic faith because a person will certainly be lost unless he adheres to the whole faith in its entirety.

This is what the catholic faith teaches:

We worship one God in Trinity, and we worship the Trinity in unity. We distinguish between the Persons, but we do not divide the substance because the Father is a distinct Person; the Son is a distinct Person; and the Holy Spirit is a distinct Person. Yet, the Father and the Son and the Holy Spirit are one divine being, having equal glory and coeternal majesty.

What the Father is, the Son is, and the Holy Spirit is. The Father is uncreated, the Son is uncreated, and the Holy Spirit is uncreated. The Father is boundless, the Son is boundless, and the Holy Spirit is boundless. The Father is eternal, the Son is eternal, and the Holy Spirit is eternal. And yet, there are not three eternal beings, but one eternal being. And there are neither three uncreated beings, nor three boundless beings, but one uncreated being and one boundless being. In the same way, the Father is omnipotent, the Son is omnipotent, and the Holy Spirit is omnipotent. Yet, there are not three omnipotent beings, but one omnipotent being.

So the Father is God, the Son is God, and the Holy Spirit is God; and yet, there are not three gods, but one God. The Father is Lord, the Son is Lord, and the Holy Spirit is Lord; and yet, there are not three lords, but one Lord. Because just as we are compelled by the Christian truth to profess each of the Persons individually as God, we are also prohibited by the catholic religion to say that there are three gods or three lords.

The Father is not made by anyone, neither created by anyone nor born from anyone. The Son is of the Father alone. The Son is not made, nor created, but is born from the Father alone. The Holy Spirit from both the Father and the Son. The Holy Spirit is not made, neither created, nor born, but proceeds from. There is, then, one Father, not three fathers; one Son, not three sons; one Holy Spirit, not three holy spirits. Not one of the members in this Trinity is before or after the others, neither are any greater or less than any of the others, but all three Persons are co-eternal and coequal with one another. So that, as has already been said, we worship unity in the Trinity and the Trinity in unity. This, then, is what anyone who wants to be saved must believe about the Trinity.

It is also necessary for eternal salvation that a person faithfully believes in the incarnation of our Lord Jesus Christ.

The true faith is this:

We believe and profess that our Lord Jesus Christ, the Son of God, is both God and human. As God, he was born from the substance of the Father before the creation of the world; as human, he was born in the world from the substance of his mother. He is perfect God and perfect human, having a rational soul and human flesh. He is equal to the Father in his divinity, but he is inferior to the Father in his humanity.

Although he is God and human, he is not two, but one Christ. And he is one, not because his divinity was changed into flesh, but because his humanity was assumed to God. He is one, not at all because of the mingling of substances, but because he is one person. Just as a rational soul and flesh are one man, so God and man are one Christ. He died for our salvation, descended to the realm of the dead, was resurrected from the dead on the third day, ascended into heaven, sits at the right hand of God the All-Powerful Father, and from there he will come to judge the living and the dead. At his coming, all people will rise again with their own bodies; and they will give an accounting of their lives. Those who have done good will go into eternal

life; those who have done evil will go into everlasting
fire.

This is the catholic faith that a person must faithfully
and firmly believe or else that person cannot be saved.

These councils and creeds lay out the basis of the
Catholic faith. These are the essence of Old Catholic faith.
These are, as far as Old Catholics are concerned, the
"infallible" and reliable statements of the Church.

WHAT DO OLD CATHOLICS BELIEVE?

This Is the Faith of the Old Catholic Church as Defined by Holy Scripture, Holy Tradition, Ecumenical Councils, and the Documents of the Old Catholic Church:

1. We believe in The Holy Trinity—that God is Father, Son, and Holy Spirit.

2. We believe that everything that exists was created by God.

3. We believe that Jesus Christ is the second person of the Holy Trinity, who came in the flesh.

4. We believe that Jesus Christ is the clear image of who God is.

5. We believe that Jesus Christ died on the cross to atone for sin and rose from the dead in accordance with the Scriptures.

6. We believe that Jesus is coming again to establish the eternal Kingdom of God on the earth.

7. We believe that the Holy Spirit has guided the Catholic Church in all her doctrines and dogmas.

8. We believe that the term "Catholic Church" has always meant what the church has taught and

affirmed by all Christians everywhere in all times and places.

9. We reject the new doctrine that the word "Catholic" means being in union with the Bishop of Rome.

10. We believe in One, Holy, Catholic, and Apostolic Church.

11. We believe baptism washes away original sin.

12. We believe in the resurrection of the dead.

13. We believe in the three historic creeds: Nicene, Apostles, and Athanasian.

14. We believe that the Catholic faith was established by Ecumenical Councils guided by the Holy Spirit.

15. We believe that there were seven Ecumenical Councils of the whole church:

> *The Council of Nicaea (325),*
> *The Council of Constantinople (381),*
> *The Council of Ephesus (431),*
> *The Council of Chalcedon (451),*
> *The Second Council of Constantinople (453),*
> *The Third Council of Constantinople (680-681),*
> *The Second Council of Nicaea (787).*

16. We believe that all other "Councils" after 1054 were not Ecumenical Councils, since the whole church did not meet together, but that they were Synods of a part of the whole church; therefore, their decisions are not binding on the whole church.

17. We believe that the Bible is the inspired Word of God.

18. We believe that the apocryphal or deuterocanonical books of the Old Testament are not of the same canonicity as the books contained in the Hebrew Canon – they are good for personal edification and spiritual growth, but not for doctrine.

19. We believe that the Bible in the original languages is superior to any one translation.

20. We believe that the Bible should be read in the common language that is understood by the people (English in England, French in France, German in Germany, etc.).

21. We believe that the Bible is the primary source for our faith, but we also accept the Holy Tradition as

passed down by the Apostles through teaching, documents of the early Church, and Ecumenical Councils.

22. We believe in and maintain Apostolic Succession.

23. We Believe in the guidance of the Early Church Fathers as part of Holy Tradition.

24. We believe that the liturgy of the church should be conducted in the common language that is understood by the people.

25. We believe that faith and works are required of us by God (because we do what we believe).

26. We believe that no amount of good deeds can earn salvation. Salvation comes by God's grace through Jesus Christ.

27. We respect the Saints of the church, but we do not believe that they have earned some sort of extra salvation that can be transferred to others.

28. We believe in seven Sacraments of the church:

Baptism
Confirmation
Holy Eucharist

Anointing of the Sick
Absolution--Confession and Reconciliation
Marriage
Holy Orders

29. We believe that the Sacraments of baptism and the
    Eucharist are the primary Sacraments of the
    church.

30. We believe that the Eucharistic celebration is not a
    continual sacrifice, or a re-sacrifice of Christ, but its
    sacrificial character consists in that it is a
    permanent memorial of Christ's sacrifice that was
    offered once forever on the cross.

31. We believe in the real presence of Christ in the
    Eucharist – that the bread and wine are the Body
    and Blood of Christ.

32. We believe that the Sacrament of the Eucharist is
    open to all who are baptized, regardless of their
    personal views regarding the character of the
    Eucharist.

33. We believe that celibacy for those in Holy Orders is
    a personal decision and voluntary, not required.

34. We believe that the practice of confession of sins
    before the congregation or a Priest is a Sacrament

that has been passed down to us by the Catholic
Church, but it is not required for forgiveness of
sins.

35. We believe that the doctrines of the Immaculate
Conception of the Blessed Virgin Mary is a new
teaching that has crept into the church and is not
the product of the Catholic Church, neither does it
reflect the teaching of the Catholic Church;
therefore, it is a new idea that crept into the
church and is neither binding on the Catholic
Church to observe, nor is it binding on any person
to accept.

36. We believe that the doctrine of the infallibility of
the Bishop of Rome is a new teaching that has
crept into the church and is not the product of the
Catholic Church, neither does it reflect the teaching
of the Catholic Church; therefore, it is a new idea
that crept into the church and is neither binding on
the Catholic Church to observe, nor is it binding on
any person to accept.

37. We believe that the pope, as Bishop of Rome, is an
heir to the apostolic authority and ministry of the
Apostles; therefore, the Bishop of Rome is
respected.

38. We believe that all Bishops hold equal apostolic calling and authority and no one See is above any other in authority.

39. We believe that the idea that the Bishop of Rome is the ruler of the church is not in keeping with the Catholic Church, but it is a new idea that crept into the church and is neither binding on the Catholic Church to observe, nor is it binding on any person to accept.

40. We believe that the use of "Catholic" for only those who are in full communion with the Bishop of Rome as ruler of the church is not in keeping with the Catholic Church, the Seven Ecumenical Councils, Holy Tradition, or Scripture of the Catholic Church. Therefore, it is a new idea that crept into the church and is neither binding on the Catholic Church to observe, nor is it binding on any person to accept.

41. We believe that marriage is a Sacrament, but divorce and remarriage are realities. We do not believe that divorce is the "unforgivable sin," neither do we believe that divorce should bar anyone from the ministry and Sacraments of the church.

42. We believe contraception is a personal decision.

43. We believe in teaching what the whole church has always taught everywhere. We do not teach theological speculation, new and controversial doctrines, neither do we believe in debating or arguing them with anyone.

44. We believe that the church cannot compel anyone to believe anything and that it is not the role of the church to impose "faith" on anyone, in and out of the church.

45. We believe the role of the clergy is to guide morality and faith by being examples, not by being authoritarians. The clergy serves the church; they do not impose their will on it.

46. We believe that the Catholic Church combats unbelief and religious indifference by faithfully professing the doctrine of Jesus Christ, by refusing to admit human error into the teaching of the Catholic Church, by weeding out any abuses of the church, and by the clergy living simple lives of faith that serve as examples to others.

Some Old Catholics jurisdictions also teach the following, and many Old Catholics in all jurisdictions may personally believe the following. Nevertheless, the following are not beliefs universally shared by Old

Catholics and no Old Catholic is required to believe the following.

47. We believe in the responsible stewardship of our planet.

48. We believe that there is nothing in the teaching of the Catholic Church as expressed in her Holy Tradition and the Seven Ecumenical Councils that impedes anyone from participating in Holy Orders; therefore, *ALL* Holy Orders are open to men and women regardless of marital state or sexual orientation, or gender identity.

49. We believe in, and advocate for, the full inclusion of *LGBT* persons in the church and in society.

50. We believe in and support marriage equality, trusting that God celebrates the love between two consenting adults, despite gender or any other variables including physical or sexual ability.

51. We believe in being truly Pro-Life, in that we consider all life to be sacred and we believe that Pro-Life has to do with quality of life for all people; therefore, we are pro-education, anti-poverty, anti-violence, anti-war, pro-health care, and oppose torture and the death penalty. We also believe that Pro-Choice is not incompatible with any of this.

Pro-Life cannot be limited to "Pro-Birth" and Pro-Choice does not mean "Pro-Abortion."

Many Old Catholics also accept the following statements:

A. All persons who have received a Trinitarian baptism are by virtue of that baptism Christians and Disciples of Christ.

B. All persons who have received a Trinitarian baptism and adhere to the ancient Catholic faith as expressed by the Nicene Creed are Catholics.

C. All persons who adhere to the full Catholic faith as received by the church until the Schism of A.D. 1054 are Old Catholics, in the fullness of the Catholic faith.

D. All Christians holding the fullness of the Catholic and Apostolic faith, regardless of their church affiliation, are regarded as being in communion with us, and may be received in fellowship and admitted to the sacraments and receive pastoral care.

The first forty-six points are generally shared by all Old Catholics. Yet, even in these there may be some variations, at least in language or expression. The last few points are not shared by every Old Catholic Church. A tiny minority do not ordain women. Some do not ordain homosexuals or perform same-sex marriages. And that is fine. It is their right to believe as they do on these matters. In our essential beliefs we have unity; in our non-essential beliefs we show liberty; and in all our beliefs we show charity.

In the Old Catholic Church, bishops and priests do not rule or impose their will on anyone. They serve as examples. There is a Catholic faith, a faith that has been passed down from the very beginning of the Church to the present, and we in the Old Catholic Church maintain that faith. Yet, there is also a variety of expression for that faith. It is not our job as clergy to impose belief or faith on anyone, but to serve others, guide where we can, and accept those who express their Catholic faith differently.

OLD & ROMAN CATHOLICS AT A GLANCE

Papal Infallibility

Old Catholic: Pope Is Not Infallible at All

Roman Catholic: Pope Is Infallible on Matters of Doctrine

Authority of the Pope

Old Catholic: the Pope Is the Bishop of Rome

Roman Catholic: the Pope Is the Ruling Official of the Church

Authority of Bishops

Old Catholic: All Bishops Are Equally Apostolic

Roman Catholic: All Bishops Are under the Authority of the Pope

Celibacy

Old Catholic: Not Required by Clergy

Roman Catholic: Required by Clergy

Ordination of Women

Old Catholic: Yes[7]

Roman Catholic: No

Use of Contraception

Old Catholic: Personal Choice

Roman Catholic: a Serious Sin

Sin

Old Catholic: All Sin Is Potentially Grave

Roman Catholic: Two Types of Sin (Venial and Mortal)

When Sin Is Forgiven

Old Catholic: When Acknowledged and Asked to Be
Forgiven (Prayer)

Roman Catholic: When Confessed to a Priest and Given
Absolution

Personal Confession to a Priest

Old Catholic: Not Required, but Encouraged for
Spiritual Growth and Humility

Roman Catholic: Required for Sins to Be Forgiven

---

[7]There are a few Old Catholic Communions that do not
ordain women; Some Old Catholic Communions do not ordain
GLBT or perform same-sex unions.

Divorce

Old Catholic: It Happens

Roman Catholic: Not Allowed

Remarriage after Divorce

Old Catholic: Yes

Roman Catholic: No

Who May Partake of the Eucharist

Old Catholic: All Baptized Christians

Roman Catholic: Only Roman Catholics

Number of Sacraments

Old Catholic: Seven

Roman Catholic: Seven

Real Presence of Christ in the Eucharist

Old Catholic: Yes

Roman Catholic: Yes

Historic Catholic Doctrines

Old Catholic: Yes

Roman Catholic: No -- Have Adopted New Doctrines

Catholic Liturgy

Old Catholic: Yes

Roman Catholic: Yes

Holy Orders Open to Homosexuals

Old Catholic: Yes[8]

Roman Catholic: No

Performs Same-Sex Marriage[9]

Old Catholic: Yes

Roman Catholic: No

Open and Affirming of GLBT[10]

Old Catholic: Yes

Roman Catholic: No

There may be other differences and similarities as well.
Many of these have to do with customs and matters of

---

[8] Not every Old Catholic Communion is open and affirming
of GLBT.

[9] Not every Old Catholic Communion performs same-sex
marriages.

discipline. Other than the differences listed, most Old Catholics and Roman Catholics mostly share the same beliefs in doctrine. The two notable exceptions are the doctrines of the Immaculate Conceptions and the doctrine of Papal Infallibility. Old Catholics also are not subject to the authority of the Bishop of Rome as the head of the whole church, but respects the Bishop of Rome because, as a bishop, he holds Apostolic Authority, but that authority is no more or no less than any other bishop.

---

[10]Not every Old Catholic Communion is open and affirming of GLBT.

HISTORIC DOCUMENTS OF THE OLD CATHOLIC CHURCH

After the bishops who walked out of the First Vatican Council went to the Catholic Church in the Netherlands and asked to join, they came up with fourteen points where they could all agree. These have become one of the important historical documents of the Old Catholic Church. The text of the theses is in bold type, and any commentary that I have added will be written in italics.

The Fourteen Theses of the Old Catholic Union Conference at Bonn (September 14-16, 1874)

I. **We agree that the apocryphal or deuterocanonical books of the Old Testament are not of the same canonicity as the books contained in the Hebrew Canon.** *(Those seven additional books that we Catholics use are historically part of the Bible, but we agree that even though they are good for inspiration and personal edification, they may not be reliable for establishing doctrine.)*

II. **We agree that no translation of Holy Scripture can claim an authority superior to that of the original text.** *(There is no perfect translation of the Bible to be used. The Original Hebrew or Greek is superior to any translation.)*

III.   **We agree that the reading of Holy Scripture in the vulgar tongue cannot be lawfully forbidden.** *(There's no reason not to read the Bible in the language everyone understands, i.e. e. English in England, French in France, German in Germany, etc. This was back in the days when only Latin was used in church and the Bible was said to only be able to be read in Latin.)*

IV.   **We agree that, in general, it is more fitting, and in accordance with the spirit of the Church, that the Liturgy should be in the tongue understood by the people.** *(No more Latin Mass, but English Mass in England and so on. These two points [III and IV] proposed the radical idea that people should be able to understand what's going on in church and be able to understand the Bible.)*

V.   **We agree that Faith working by Love, not Faith without Love, is the means and condition of Man's justification before God.** *(Faith isn't just a warm fuzzy feeling in your heart, but it is expressed in deeds, as is love. You do what you believe; if you don't do it, you don't believe it.)*

VI.   **Salvation cannot be merited by "merit of condignity," because there is no proportion between the infinite worth of salvation promised by God and the finite worth of man's works.** *(This is a fancy way of saying that our salvation is not a reward for the good deeds we do. We don't earn salvation because we can never earn it – our deeds are but simple drops in the ocean of God's grace and love.)*

VII.   **We agree that the doctrine of *"opera supererogationis"* and of a *"thesaurus meritorium sanctorum,"* i.e., that the overflowing merits of the Saints can be transferred to others, either by the rulers of the Church, or by the authors of the good works themselves, is untenable.** *(This says that even if our good deeds could save us, those who were really good like the saints cannot transfer the extra-salvation they may have earned by their good deeds. I know it sounds crazy but there was an idea that the saints, through their good works, had an overabundance of the effect of those good works, and since they didn't need it, they could transfer it to others. This thesis says that there is nothing to support that idea.)*

VIII.   1) **We acknowledge that the number of sacraments was fixed at seven, first in the twelfth century, and then was received into the general teaching of the Church, not as a tradition coming down from the Apostles or from the earliest of times, but as the result of theological speculation.** *(There are seven Sacraments, but that number was determined by the church by theologians and not because Jesus, St. Peter or any other Apostle, said that there are seven Sacraments.)*

2) **Catholic theologians acknowledge, and we acknowledge with them, that Baptism and the Eucharist are "principalia, praecipus, eximia salutis nostrae sacramenta."** *(Out of the seven Sacraments, the primary Sacraments are Baptism and the Eucharist. Most Protestants claim they are the only Sacraments, and we agree that they are the most important, but we will stick with the tradition of the church until there is a valid reason not to.)*

IX.   1) **The Holy Scriptures being recognized as the primary rule of Faith, we agree that the genuine tradition, i.e. the unbroken transmission partly oral, partly in writing of the doctrine delivered by Christ and the Apostles is an authoritative source of teaching for all successive generations of Christians. This tradition is partly to be found in the consensus of the great ecclesiastical bodies standing in historical continuity with the primitive Church, partly to be gathered by scientific method from the written documents of all centuries.** *(Yes, we agree that the Bible is the primary source for understanding our faith, but we also agree that our understanding of the Bible comes out of our tradition. The tradition we use is the long tradition of the Catholic Church that has been left for us in documents and church councils. The Catholic Church existed before the Bible was written, so the Bible itself is part of the tradition of the church. So we use the tradition to understand the Bible.)*

2) **We acknowledge that the Church of England; and the Churches derived through her, have maintained unbroken the Episcopal succession.** (The Church of England and the churches that flow from her [*i.e.* The Episcopal Church] are valid expressions of the Catholic faith.)

X.   **We reject the new Roman doctrine of the Immaculate Conception of the Blessed Virgin Mary, as being contrary to the tradition of the first thirteen centuries, according to which Christ alone is conceived without sin.** (Celebrate and believe them if you want, but you are not required to accept them and the Old Catholic Church maintains that they are new and spurious doctrines that have crept into the Church.)

XI.   **We agree that the practice of confession of sins before the congregation or a Priest, together with the exercise of the power of the keys, has come down to us from the primitive Church, and that, purged from abuses and free from constraint, it should be preserved in the Church.** *(Confession is good for you. Do it! Besides, the absolution you receive is valid for all your sins, even if you are only confessing or aware of a few of them.)*

XII.   **We agree that "indulgences" can only refer to penalties actually imposed by the Church herself.** *(Indulgences are situations where the church shortens or ends the time one spends in purgatory. The church got a little careless with them and they were sold as "get out of hell free cards" that robbed the poor of their money and made a lot of money for the church. This is saying that the church can only grant a remission of temporal punishment on those things that the church itself decided is bad. I think an example would be eating meat on Friday for those who are old enough to remember when that was considered a sin. There is nothing in the Bible or the doctrine to make that a sin. It was a means of generating business for fish merchants during The Middle Ages. So, the church can only limit the punishment someone receives for violating a rule that the church made up.)*

XIII.   **We acknowledge that the practice of the commemoration of the faithful departed, i.e. the calling down of a richer outpouring of Christ's grace upon them, has come down to us from the primitive Church, and is to be preserved in the Church.** (The Church has encouraged prayer for the dead from the earliest times as an act of Christian charity. "If we had no care for the dead," Augustine noted, "we would not be in the habit of praying for them." Monastic communities began to mark an annual day of prayer for the departed members. In the middle of the 11th century, Saint Odilo, abbot of Cluny, France, decreed that all Cluniac monasteries offer special prayers and sing the Office for the Dead on November 2, the day after the feast of All Saints.)

XIV.   1) **The Eucharistic celebration in the Church is not a continuous repetition or renewal of the propitiatory sacrifice offered once forever by Christ upon the cross; but its sacrificial character consists in this, that it is the permanent memorial of it, and a representation and presentation on earth of that one oblation of Christ for the salvation of redeemed mankind, which according to the Epistle to the Hebrews (9:11, 12), is continuously presented in heaven by Christ, who now appears in the presence of God for us (9:24).**(Christ is not continually sacrificed at the celebration of the Eucharist. The Eucharist is sacrificial in nature because it commemorates the sacrificed made by Christ once for all time.

2) **While this is the character of the Eucharist in reference to the sacrifice of Christ, it is also a sacred feast, wherein the faithful, receiving the Body and Blood of our Lord, have communion one with another (I Cor. 10:17).** *(The real presence of Christ in the Eucharist is affirmed; however, it is never defined. The real presence is affirmed by the idea that all who share the Eucharist are in communion with each other. The real presence of the Eucharist unites all the faithful into one Body. This thesis will be repeated in the Eight Utrecht Declarations.)*

DECLARATIONS OF UTRECHT

Later the Old Catholic leadership met together again and came up with eight more things to agree on: although, some of it was simply agreeing on what they already agreed to in the past. What follows is not the actual Utrecht Declarations, but a summary of what they mean and how they define the Old Catholic faith.

THE ESSENCE OF THE PROFESSION OF FAITH, OR DECLARATION, FORMULATED BY THE OLD CATHOLIC BISHOPS ASSEMBLED AT UTRECHT

(SEPTEMBER 24th, 1889)

CATHOLIC BUT NOT ROMAN, ORTHODOX BUT
NOT EASTERN

I. WHAT IT MEANS TO BE "CATHOLIC"

We adhere to the Catholic faith in that we adhere to what has always been believed everywhere by all the faithful. That is what "catholic" means. So we profess the faith as expressed by the Seven Ecumenical Councils of the undivided church that met during the first thousand years.

II. INFALIBILITY OF THE BISHOP OF ROME

Because of what has been stated in the first declaration, we reject the so-called First Vatican "council" which formalized the infallibility and universal bishopric of the Bishop of Rome. These decrees contradict the tradition of the church and its constitution by extending universal authority and a number of additional powers over all the faithful. Nevertheless, we do not deny that the ancient church spoke of the importance of the See of Rome and even called the Bishop of Rome the first among equals.

III. THE DOCTRINE OF THE IMMACULATE CONCEPTION

We reject the dogma of the Immaculate Conception. It contradicts the Holy Scriptures and contradicts the tradition of the church throughout the centuries.

IV. THEOLOGICAL ERRORS

We reject other Encyclicals, Bulls, and other documents published by the Bishop of Rome in recent times. We reject them on points where they contradict the doctrine of the primitive church, and we do not recognize them as binding on the consciences of the faithful. We also renew the ancient protests of the Catholic Church of Holland against the errors of the Roman Curia and against Rome's attacks against the rights of national churches.

V. THE COUNCIL OF TRENT

We refuse to accept the decrees issued by the Council of Trent regarding discipline. We accept the dogmatic decisions of that council only so far as they are in harmony with the teaching of the primitive church (as expressed in the Ecumenical Councils).

VI. THE HOLY EUCHARIST

The Holy Eucharist has always been the true central point of Catholic worship. We declare that we maintain with perfect fidelity the ancient Catholic doctrine concerning the Sacrament because we believe that we receive the Body and Blood of our Savior Jesus Christ under the species of bread and wine.

The Eucharistic celebration in the church is neither a continual repetition of Christ's sacrifice on the cross, nor is it a renewal of that sacrifice. That sacrifice was offered once for all.

The Eucharist is a sacrifice in that it is the perpetual commemoration of the sacrifice offered upon the cross. It is the act that represents on earth in an appropriate manner of the one offering Jesus Christ makes in heaven for the salvation of redeemed humanity by appearing for us in the presence of God. ((according to Heb. 9:11-12 and Heb. 9:24).

So the character of the Eucharist is understood as a sacrificial feast by which all the faithful who receive the Body and Blood of our Savior enter into communion with one another (I Cor. 10:17).

VII. CATHOLIC TEACHINGS

We hope the Catholic theologians can maintain the faith of the undivided Church and establish and agreement that settles controversial matters that have kept the church divided. We exhort the priest of our jurisdiction to teach in their preaching and their instruction to the young the essential Christian truths that all Christians have everywhere always professed. We exhort them to avoid discussing and teaching controversial doctrines. We also encourage our priest to set an example of truth and charity to the members of the church by their words and actions.

VIII. COMBATING HERESY

The great evils of our day are unbelief and religious indifference. We believe that we can effectively combat these evils by: (1) faithfully professing the doctrine of Jesus Christ, (2) by refusing to admit human error into the teaching of the Catholic Church, and (3) by laying aside the abuses of the church, and the worldly tendencies of the hierarchy of the church.

WHY HAVE I NEVER HEARD OF THE OLD CATHOLIC CHURCH BEFORE NOW?

At some point in the conversation, someone will invariably say to me: "Wow! That's interesting! But why have I never heard of The Old Catholic Church before now?" That is a good question and it has a very simple answer. The Old Catholic Church in the United States has always been fragmented.

In most other nations that has a significant Old Catholic presence, those churches are organized into a national structure. One of the early decisions of the Old Catholic Church was that the authority over the church within any nation would not extend beyond that nation. This means that all Old Catholic Churches within each nation are autonomous and independent from every other nation.

The Union of Utrecht is the first Old Catholic Church, but Utrecht did not become the Rome of the Old Catholic Church. The Church in the Netherlands cannot tell the Church in Mexico how to be the Church. Neither can the Church in Mexico tell the Union of Utrecht how to be Old Catholic. Each Church in each nation is independent of the Old Catholic Churches in other nations. They may enter into a "union" or be in communion with each other if they wish, but even then, they cannot dictate how to be Old

Catholic. This was demonstrated in past years when the Polish National Churches in the United States formally broke away from the Union of Utrecht over the issues of ordaining women and homosexuals.

Another reason why you may have never heard of the Old Catholic Church is that it does not have to be a national church. It can be smaller. There may be an Old Catholic Church in Canada and in Mexico and in Australia, but there is no single national Old Catholic Church in the United States. There are hundreds of Old Catholic Churches in the United States. This is the result of independent missionaries setting up independent Old Catholic Communities in the United States. It is the result of those independent communities not wanting to give up its little piece of its kingdom, keeping the communities divided in structure. It is also the result of infighting of many of those communities, which, like many churches, argue, break into factions, and split.

Many of us in the Old Catholic Church dream of a time when the Old Catholic Churches in the United States would form a larger, national structure. Attempts have been made in the past to do just that. Nevertheless, these attempts fail for some reason or another.

I LIKE WHAT I HAVE READ! WHAT DO I DO NOW?

I travel a lot as an Old Catholic priest. I travel hundreds of miles to officiate weddings, baptize, and perform ministry however is required. People usually have a lot of questions about the Old Catholic Church. Most the most frequent questions have been addressed in the preceding pages. At this point in the conversation, many people ask me how they can find an Old Catholic Church near them.

That is a tricky question to answer because of what I have already mentioned about the Old Catholic Church in the United States being fragmented. There are hundreds of Old Catholic Communions. So, the only advice I can offer is to get online if you are able and start searching. In the following pages I will provide a list of Old Catholic Churches to help in your search if that is what you decide.

Yet, and this may sound strange, my goal is not to get you to leave your church and join the Old Catholic Church. My question for you would be to ask why you want to find an Old Catholic Church. If you attend a Roman Catholic Church and are upset about political statements, or birth control, or some other issue, do not leave the church. Let them know that you know about the Old Catholic Church– a church that has valid Apostolic Succession, that has valid Sacraments, that is 100% Catholic in the true meaning of the word, that believes that birth control is a personal decision, and accepts that divorce is not an unforgiveable sin, that also offers the Sacraments to all people, regardless of whether they are Roman Catholic, Old Catholic, Eastern Orthodox, Anglican, or any other flavor of Catholic. The Roman Catholic Church is a powerful institution. It has a lot of wealth and it has a lot of members. But the most powerful tool it has is convincing its members that the Roman Catholic Church is the only validly Catholic Church around. The only way to effect change within the Roman Catholic Church (if that is what you desire) is to let the Roman Catholic Church know that you have discovered that there are Old Catholics who think and believe more like you do than the Roman Catholic Church seems to.

The truth is that most American Roman Catholics believe what Old Catholics believe about most issues. Most American Roman Catholics believe that clergy should be able to marry. Most American Roman Catholics believe that it is none of the Church's business if they use birth control or contraception. Most American Roman Catholics accept that people are gay and that many of those people believe that homosexuals should be able to marry like anyone else. Many American Roman Catholics believe that the fact that they are divorced should not bar them from receiving Sacraments.

The past two Presidential elections have shown that Roman Catholics vote like the population as a whole. You can take the popular vote of the nation and compare it with the way Roman Catholics voted and the numbers are the same. This means that most American Roman Catholics are moderates in their theology, their politics, and in most other areas of their lives. Some of them are Liberal or Progressive. Some of them are Conservative. Most Conservative Roman Catholics are happy in their church. Many Moderate Roman Catholics are becoming increasingly uncomfortable with a Conservative agenda that seems more political than religious. And Progressives are either fleeing the Roman Catholic Church, or they are gritting their teeth as they are told political spin disguised as faith.

But even still, give your church a chance. Let your priest, your bishop, let fellow parishioners know that you are aware of the Old Catholic Church and you like what you have heard. The Roman Catholic Church will get the message. It may take time, but they will get it.

None of this is meant to bash or denigrate the Roman Catholic Church in any way. I actually am very fond of the Roman Catholic Church and I frequently attend, as a guest, a Roman Catholic Church around the corner from my home since there is no Old Catholic community close by. I sometimes attend the Episcopal Church near my home, and sometimes another tradition altogether. As I said, Old Catholics are generally ecumenical and work and pray well with others. It is not an agenda of Old Catholicism to critique or malign the Roman Catholic Church. If you meet an Old Catholic priest, bishop, or anyone else who is hostile at the Roman Catholic Church to the point in which they are derogatory, flee! That person is not representing the views or stance of The Old Catholic Church, but merely expressing his or her own bigotries.

The Old Catholic Church from its inception has encouraged its clergy not to engage in theological speculation or debate, but merely to adhere to those Catholic teachings that have been passed down. Clergy and laity are allowed to believe what they want to about most things, but whatever we may decide to believe, we should be careful that those beliefs are expressed with love. After all, God is love; therefore, if we are not doing something with love, we are not doing it for God. Love is not what God does. Love is what God is!

So if you have a church home that you like, even though you may be frustrated at times with what it is saying about issues that are important to you. My counsel would be to do your best to remain a faithful member of that church and see if you can foster the change you desire. If, however, you have avoided church for a while, or if you do not think you can continue in the church you are in, then by all means, check out the Old Catholic Church. Use the list provided in this book to find one that sounds like something you like, and search to see if they have a church near you. If there is no Old Catholic Church around, then try an Episcopal Church.

Of course, you can always ask me questions. I have a presence on Facebook, Twitter, and other social media. I enjoy teaching about the Old Catholic Church.

May God bless you on your journey!

APPENDIX I: TABLE OF APOSTOLIC SUCCESSION OF THE AUTHOR

From

Jesus Christ

To

The Apostles

Peter, James, John, Andrew, Simon, Matthew, Jude,

Bartholomew, Phillip, James, Thomas,

And Their Successors,

The Bishops of the One, Holy, Catholic and Apostolic
Church

AD 33 to AD 1566

On 12 March, 1566

Cardinal Scipione Rebiba,

Consecrated

Giulio Antonio Santorio,

Who on 7 September 1586

Consecrated

Girolamo Bernerio, O.P.,

Who on 4 April 1604

Consecrated

Galeazzo Sanvitale,

Who on 2 May 1621

Consecrated

Ludovico Ludovisi,

Who on 12 June 1622

Consecrated

Luigi Caetani,

Who on 7 October 1630

Consecrated

Giovanni Battista Scannaroli,

Who on 24 October 1655

Consecrated

Antonio Cardinal Barberini

Who, as Archbishop of Rheims, 1657

Consecrated

Charleas Maurice Latellier,

Who on November 12, 1668

Consecrated

James Benigne Bossuet

Who on September 21, 1670

Consecrated

James Goydon De Matignon,

Who on February 12, 1719
Consecrated

Dominic M. Varlet,
Who on October 17, 1739
Consecrated

Peter John Meindaerts,
Who on July 11, 1745
Consecrated

John Van Stiphout,
Who on February 7, 1768
Consecrated

Walter Michael Van Nieuwenhuizen,
Who on June 21, 1778
Consecrated

Adrian Broekman,
Who on November 7, 1805
Consecrated

John James Van Rhijin,
Who Consecrated

Gilbert De Jong,
Who on April 24, 1814
Consecrated

Willibrod Van Os,
Who on April 22, 1819
Consecrated

John Bon,
Who on June 14, 1825
Consecrated

John Van Santen,
Who on July 17, 1854
Consecrated

Herman Heykamp,
Who on August 11, 1873
Consecrated

Gaspard John Rinkel,
Who on May 11, 1872
Consecrated

Gerard Gul,
Who on April 28, 1908
Consecrated

Arnold Harris Mathew,
Who on June 29, 1913
Consecrated

The Prince Bishopêêde Landas Berghes,
Who on October 4, 1916
Consecrated

Henry Carmel Carfora
Who on December 8, 1940
Consecrated

Francis Xavier Resch
Who on June 17, 1945
Consecrated

Earl Anglin Lawrence James
Who on December 25, 1950
Consecrated

Grant Timothy Billet
Who on October 23, 1979
Consecrated

Norman Richard Parr
Who on July 14, 1991
Consecrated

Maurice Darryl Mccormick,
Who Ordained

R. Joseph Owles

Deacon on February 28, 1999;

Priest on July 11, 1999.

APPENDIX II: LIST OF OLD CATHOLIC CHURCHES

Utrecht Union

Member churches

Union of Utrecht **of the Old Catholic Churches**

- Old Catholic Church of the Netherlands

- Catholic Diocese of the Old Catholics in Germany

- Christian Catholic Church of Switzerland

- Old Catholic Church of Austria

- Old Catholic Church of the Czech Republic

Dependent jurisdictions

- Old Catholic Mission in France

- Old Catholic Church in Italy

- Old Catholic Church in Sweden and Denmark

- Old Catholic Church of Croatia[citation needed]

- Polish Catholic Church in Canada

-

Ecclesial jurisdiction in full communion with Utrecht

- Old Catholic Confederation of the Oratory of St. Augustine is an Old Catholic society of priests within the Episcopal Church and, therefore, in full communion with the See of Utrecht.

United States and Canada: dioceses, parishes and missions

- Diocese of St. Benedict Old Catholic Church

- Corpus Christi Ecumenical Fellowship

Churches which ordain women and LGBT people

- Parishes not in communion with Old Catholic jurisdictions in the United States

- Church of the Holy Paraclete (Providence, RI)

- Diocese of California American Catholic Church (Western US, California)

- Christ's Catholic Church: An Ecumenical Free Catholic Communion in the Old Catholic Tradition *Structured nationally and shepherded by three Convening Bishops, Brian Ernest Brown, Jane Harper, and Andrew Eugene Kyle*

- Diocese of the Epiphany Bp. David Cronan - Chicago, Illinois affiliated with Christ's Catholic Church

- Diocese of Saint John the Evangelist Bp. Dave Pflueger - Tacoma, Washington affiliated with Christ's Catholic Church

- Order of the Friends of Jeshua Bp. Lee Allen Petersen and Bp. Linda Marie Nelson - Weatherford, Texas affiliated with Christ's Catholic Church

- Order of the Shepherd's Heart Bp. Brian Ernest Brown - Hollister, Missouri affiliated with Christ's Catholic Church

- Whithorn School of Theology Seminary - Hollister, Missouri affiliated with Christ's Catholic Church

- Ecumenical Catholic Church (Archbishop Mark Shirilau, Primate)

- Conference of North American Old Catholic Bishops - *build upon initiative of the Union of Utrecht, would become one church and a member of the Union.* The churches which were members of the Conference have now merged as one church and is now known as The Old

Catholic Church, Province of the United States (TOCCUSA) The Old Catholic Church, Province of the United States

- American Catholic Church in New England divided into two dioceses: the Old Catholic Diocese of New England and the Old Catholic Diocese of the Mid-Atlantic

- Heartland Old Catholic Church divided into two dioceses: Holy Cross Old Catholic Diocese of Minnesota and Old Catholic Diocese of Washington, DC

- Old Catholic Diocese of Napa (California) Old Catholic Diocese of Napa - Holy Family Old Catholic Church Fairfield, CA Holy Family

- American Apostolic Church (WI - IL - DC) - *in DC, Bishop Steven Delaney, former assistant bishop of Bishop Braun*

- American Catholic Church in the United States - (ACCUS - Lawrence J. Harms, MD - nationally structured)

- St. Padre Pio Old Catholic Church, Summerville, SC

- American National Catholic Church

- Seminary of St. John the Beloved

- Community Catholic Church of Canada Holy
  Angels Ministries

- St. Anne's Parish

- Reformed Catholic Church

- United States Old Catholic Church

- Saint Christopher Old Catholic Church

- Seminary of Saint John the Evangelist

- Catholic Apostolic Church in North America
  (CACINA - THE Catholic Apostolic Church -
  Duarte succession in USA)

- International Old Catholic Churches

- Exaltation of the Holy Cross Hermitage -
  Greenville, SC

- Saint Francis of Assisi Old Catholic Church -
  North Augusta, SC

- Walking In Faith International - Nashville, TN

- Chapel of Divine Mercy – Philippians

- The Oratory of Sts. Raphael and Dominic - Salt Lake City, UT

- Oratory of St. Jude of the Holy Spirit - Pearl, MS

- Saint Aelred Mission - Aberdeen, NJ

- Sagrada Familia Old Catholic Mission - Houston, TX

- Father Mychal Judge Outreach Ministry - Fairfax, VA

- Priory of Sts. Symeon and John - Belle, WV

- St. Padre Pio's Old Catholic Church - Madison, WI

- Ekklesia Tou Theou (Church of God) in communion with the Catholic Diocese of One Spirit. Dasmarinas City, Cavite Philippines.

- Ecclesia Apostolica Divinorum Mysteriorum ++John Kersey, Presiding Bishop

- Sophia Catholic Communion, Bishop +Laura M. Grimes, Ph.D.

- St. Junia the Apostle Chapel - Dayton, OH

General declaration of non-discrimination and
inclusiveness

- Old Catholic Church of New Utrecht, Diocese of
  St. Benedict, Glen Burnie, MD, Bishop Ed Jansen

- Old Catholic Church of New Utrecht, West Palm
  Beach, FL, Bishop. Richard Sebastian Riccardi

- Trinitarian Catholic Church, Metropolitan
  Diocese of Hope (New England, New York, New
  Jersey, Missouri, United States)

General declaration of non-discrimination -- An all-
inclusive community

- Catholic Church, Inc. Catholic Church, Inc.

- All Saints Catholic Church All Saints Catholic
  Church, Tallahassee, Florida

- Holy Angels Catholic Community Holy Angels
  Catholic Community, Winter Park, Florida

- Most Reverend Joseph Daniel Finnegan
  Ordinary of Catholic Church Inc.

- St. Faustina Old Catholic Community, Cranston,
  Rhode Island

- Most Reverend Michael R. Pierson, Auxiliary Bishop Old Catholic Church of America

- United Ecumenical Catholic Church in North America

- Franciscans of the Holy Cross (North America)

- Saints Francis and Clare United Ecumenical Catholic Church, Honolulu, Hawaii

- United Ecumenical Catholic Church in North America is part an international group of church connected with :

- The Ecumenical Christian Church (UK)

- United Ecumenical Catholic Church Metropolitan Region of Australasia

- Connected religious order : The Ecumenical Franciscan Order (Australia)

Churches which ordain women but not LGBT people

- Independent Old Catholic Church independentoldcatholicchurch.com

- Holy Angels & Saints Church

- Agnus Dei Old Catholic Society

- Old Catholic Communion in North America —
  An Old Catholic Communion open to all
  autocephalous Old Catholic jurisdictions and
  bishops seeking to establish unity.

- Old Catholic Church of North America

- Canticle of Christ Ministry An outreach ministry
  of the Old Catholic Church of North America

- Incarnation Old Catholic Mission A mission of
  the Old Catholic Church of North America

- Old Catholic Church of North America

- Old Catholic Mission of the Holy Spirit A mission
  of the Old Catholic Church of North America

- St. Dismas Ministries An outreach ministry of
  the Old Catholic Church of North America

- Ecumenical Catholic Church USA

- Old Catholic Diocese of The Holy Spirit Old
  Catholic Diocese with orthodox theology
  affiliated with the Old Catholic Communion in
  North America

- All Saints Old Catholic Church Parish in
  Tennessee

- Dove of Peace Old Catholic Church

- Saint Francis Old Catholic Mission

- Holy Trinity Old Catholic Church

Churches which do not ordain women

- Polish National Catholic Church. *It left Union of Utrecht in 2003 for that reason after the Union's Congress of Prague*

- Old Holy Catholic Church of North America (Canada - The Most Rev. Rainer Laufers)

Unclassified

- American Old Catholic Church (originally Aurora, Colorado; today, several dioceses)

- Diocese of St. Thomas Old Catholic Church An Old Catholic Church in Las Vegas, Nevada

- Old Catholic Church - de Landis Berghes Succession

- Oratory of the Common Life

- Old Catholic Diocese of Dallas (Texas)

- Restoration In Christ Church Dallas, Texas

United States and Canada: autocephalous bishoprics

- North American Old Roman Catholic Church (Landes Berghes) split after Carfora's Death in 5 bodies, among them:

- North American Old Roman Catholic Church

- North American Old Roman Catholic Church (Utrecht Succession) - Archdiocese of California

- Old Catholic Church of America

- Old Roman Catholic Church in North America

- American Catholic Church The original American Catholic Church charter established in 1915 (Los Angeles, CA)

- American Catholic Church in Nevada (Las Vegas - inclusive of gays - ordination of women and LGBT)

- American Ecumenical Catholic Church (Connecticut - Bishop Lorraine J. Bouffard)

- Apostolic Catholic Church in America (Washington state - Bishop Robert Withrow)

- Apostolic Catholic and Spiritual Church

- Caritas Catholic Church International

- Catholic Church of Americas (CapeVerdean Comm., MA - Inclusive of gays - Ordination of women and gays)

- Christ Catholic Church

- Christ Our Teacher Old Catholic Ministry (NJ - Most Rev. Benjamin M. Evans)

- Christ's Church Fellowship Inc. (Rt. Rev. David C. Holdridge, Presiding Bishop - Owensboro, Kentucky USA & Roswell, New Mexico USA, established 1988)

- CCF International (over 100 churches in over 12 nations worldwide)

- The 24/7 Christian Church Fellowship International (Christian, Catholic, & Convergent)

- Community of Charity Independent Old Catholic Church (Columbus,OH)[4]

- Community of The Good Samaritan American Independent Catholic Church Mission

- Ecumenical Catholic Church

- Ecumenical Catholic Church of Christ (ECCC) http://www.ecumenicalccc.org/

- Holy Redeemer Old Catholic Church (Crestline,OH)[5]

- Independent Catholic Church

- Independent Catholic Church of the West

- Old Catholic Church of British Columbia

- Reconciliation Old Catholic Church (Phoenix,AZ)

- Reformed Catholic Church International

- Reformed Catholic Church of America

- Servants of the Good Shepherd

- Sacred Heart of Jesus Old Roman Catholic Church (Michigan - Bishop David S. Moody, http://shjorcc.org)

- Trinitarian Catholic Church, Metropolitan Diocese of Hope (New England, New York, New Jersey, Missouri / USA)

- United Catholic Church

- United Reform Catholic Church International

- Sophia Catholic Communion (Ohio--Bishop +Laura M. Grimes)

Intercommunion:

- United American Catholic Church—In intercommunion with :

- Catholic Apostolic Church in North America (Cacina, voir plus haut)

- Contemporary Catholic Church :

- Independent Catholic Christian Church, itself with :

- Diocese of Rumney Marsh (Independent Catholics)

Old Roman Catholic Church

- Old Roman Catholic Church

Europe

- British Old Catholic Church

- Ecclesia Apostolica Jesu Christi

- *Gemeenschap van de Goede Herder*

- Old Roman Catholic Church in Europe aka Old Catholic Church in Europe

- Old Roman Catholic Church in Europ. Diocese of France.

- Old Catholic Mariavite Church

- Old Catholic Church in Slovakia

- Old Catholic Church of Ukraine

- Polish National Catholic Church in Republic of Poland

- Reformed Catholic Church in Poland

- Traditional Catholic Orthodox Church

- United Ecumenical Catholic Church Europe and the United Kingdom

- Old Holy Catholic Church Ordo Maria Apostolorum / Order of Marian Apostles

- *Église gallicane*, France

- Ecumenical Catholic Communion in Europe (Bishop Peter E. Hickman)

- ECC Austria

- ECC Belgium and Netherlands

- ECC Poland

- ECC Lithuania

- The Old Catholic Church in the United Kingdom

Liberal Catholic churches with Theosophical tenets

United States

- Liberal Catholic Church, Province of the United States of America, American branch which emphasizes Theosophical tenets

- Liberal Catholic Church International, Theosophical tenets are allowed but not emphasized

- Old Catholic, Liberal Catholic Int. (Church of St.Thomas Int.) Theosophical tenents not emphasized, members have total freedom of thought.

- Reformed Liberal Catholic Church USA province, Theosophical tenets are allowed but not emphasized

- Universal Catholic Church, Theosophical tenets are allowed by not emphasized

Europe

- The Liberal Catholic Church Overview of the entire Liberal Catholic movements, regardless of jurisdiction

- The Liberal Catholic Church International Province of Great Britain and Ireland

- The Liberal Catholic Church in the British Isles

- Liberal Catholic Apostolic Church An independent Liberal Catholic community

- The Reformed Liberal Catholic Church

- The Young Rite Ritual in an esoteric Christian tradition

Religious orders

Franciscans

- Franciscans of Divine Providence (FDP)] Canonical Religious Order of women and men of the Trinitarian Catholic Church

- Companions of Saints Francis and Dominic
  Ecumenical fraternity of vowed men and
  women

- Society of the Franciscan Servants of the Poor

- Order of Servant Franciscans (OSF), an
  ecumenical and Canonical tertiary order
  (www.tifpecusa.faithweb.com)

- ECC Franciscans of Reconciliation (OFR)

- Order Of Friars Minor

Benedictines and Cistercians

- Diocese of St. Benedict - Old Catholic Church

- Grey Robed Monks of St. Benedict - ecumenical
  Benedictine community

- Order of Port Royal - ecumenical Cistercian
  congregation

- Society of Pope Saint Anacletus - Old Catholic
  Benedictine order

- *Goedeherder Benedictijns geïnspireerde
  broedergemeenschap*

- St. Michael Old Catholic Mission

- Cistercian Province of the Sacred Hearts of Jesus and Mary

Dominican

- Old Catholic Order of Preachers (OCOP)

Others

- Little Brothers and Sisters of Jesus Caritas

- Monastery of Saint Thomas Oblate Monastery, Old Catholic Province of Our Lady of Angels

- Augustinians of the Immaculate Heart of Mary - independent Catholic religious order

- Order of the Shepherd's Heart - Christ's Catholic Church an ecumenical Celtic Catholic religious order in Hollister, Missouri.

- Order of Restoration in Christ - Old Catholic monastery in Dallas, Texas

- Oratory of the Common Life - associated with the Old Catholic Church - de Landis Berghes Succession

- Order of St. Thomas the Apostle (United States and Spain) - religious order affiliated with the Liberal Catholic Old Catholic Church Int.

ABOUT THE AUTHOR

Father R. Joseph Owles seeks to serve the Invisible God by serving those who are made in His image. He is committed to living as a disciple of Jesus Christ. He practices the Spirituality of St. Ignatius of Loyola as a "Contemplative in Action" who seeks to find God in all things. He also seeks to live the Sermon on the Mount as if it is the instruction manual for disciples of Jesus Christ. He is an author, poet, public speaker, teacher, historian, theologian, New Testament Scholar, and priest.

Father R. Joseph Owles is an Old Catholic Priest. He has served in the Independent Old Catholic Church of America and in the North American Old Catholic Church.

He has served as the Theologian to the Presiding Bishop of The North American Old Catholic Church, a Chaplain in the University of Louisville Hospital for CPE in 1995, served as the Director of Education and Youth at Anchorage Presbyterian Church, founded and is the head pastor of the Kingdom of God Catholic Church, and has worked for the headquarters of the PC (USA) serving as the Coordinator for their focus The Year With Education.

He was awarded the Alan M. Jackson Preaching Award upon completion of my M.Div. Degree.

Father R. Joseph Owles is very ecumenical and comfortable with all faiths and people. He is a College

Professor of History, Political Science, Psychology, Comparative Religions, Philosophy, World Literature, and Writing. He also has worked teaching students ranging from pre-school through college. As a student, he assisted a professor with various graduate level courses including Introduction to New Testament Greek; Introduction to the New Testament; and Greek Exegesis.

He translated the New Testament from Koine Greek into common idiomatic English, which is published under the title *The Peace Treaty: A New Translation of the New Testament for a New Millennium*, which can be found at Amazon.com, and other retailers.

He also has rendered the *Tao Te Ching* into English in *The Process of Power: Lao Tzu's Guide to Success, Politics, Governance, and Leadership*, which can be found at Amazon and other outlets.

He is also the author of *Biblical Faith: What It Is and How It Works And Christian Prosperity*, available at Amazon.

Biblical Faith: What It Is and How It Works is also available on Kindle at http://www.amazon.com/BIBLICAL-FAITH-WHAT-HOW-ebook/dp/B00EW9ZAW8

He has been published many times over in various literary journals and magazines such as The Bitter Oleander; Westview; Poetrymagazine.com, Earthworm,

Women in Cumberland County, Women in Atlantic County, and other.

You can find Father R. Joseph Owles online at:

http://kogcc.net

https://www.facebook.com/RJOwles

https://twitter.com/rjosephowles

http://www.writerscafe.org/rjowles

Made in the USA
Coppell, TX
28 November 2019